REPTILES & AMPHIBIANS

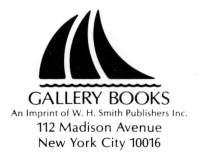

GALLERY BOOKS
An Imprint of W. H. Smith Publishers Inc.
112 Madison Avenue
New York City 10016

This edition first published in U.S.
in 1990 by Gallery Books,
an imprint of W.H. Smith Publishers, Inc.
112 Madison Avenue, New York, New York 10016

ISBN 0-8317-9591-3

Printed and bound in Spain

For rights information about the photographs in
this book please contact:

The Image Bank
111 Fifth Avenue, New York, NY 10003

Producer: Solomon M. Skolnick
Author: Scott Weidensaul
Design Concept: Leslie Ehlers
Designer: Ann-Louise Lipman
Editor: Madelyn Larsen
Production: Valerie Zars
Photo Researcher: Edward Douglas
Assistant Photo Researcher: Robert Hale

Title page: **Head to head in a bad
situation, a barking treefrog eyes a yellow
rat snake, a species which frequently preys
on treefrogs. If the snake has fed recently,
or if the day is too cool for peak activity,
the frog may well escape.**

A female snapping turtle pauses in her task, ready to cover the dozen or more eggs she has laid in a specially dug hole. Incubated by the sun, the eggs will hatch in several weeks. *Below:* The baby turtles are independent from birth, their mother having disappeared back into the pond as soon as she was done laying.

Its head pulled partway into its shell, a red-eared turtle obscures most of its major field mark. Once the standard pet store turtle, the red-eared is found naturally from the Midwest and South to New Mexico. So many "pets" have been released into the wild that it's now in many other locations. *Below:* A Florida red-bellied turtle basks in a shaft of sunlight.

ighttime on an Appalachian ridge. Moonlight filters through the canopy of oak and hickory leaves, splattering the forest floor with fragments of silver that flicker as a breeze moves the treetops. A deer mouse scurries among the fallen leaves, stopping to eat a cricket here, a shriveled greenbrier berry there. It climbs over a lichened rock, then onto a fallen log that serves as an infrequent pathway to its nest of shredded bark, in a hollow branch.

Curled beside the fallen log is a timber rattlesnake, a big female of the yellow color phase, her satiny skin marked with dark crossbands that break up her outline against the detritus of the forest floor. A day earlier, she had flowed over the leaves to this spot, where her sensitive tongue, flicking odor particles from the air, told her that mice ran along this log. She coiled here, her chin resting lightly against the wood, aimed at the top of the log.

Top to bottom: **A specialty of the Florida coast, an ornate diamondback terrapin has orange spots at the center of the large shell scutes, differentiating it from northern diamondbacks. The eastern box turtle is able to retract itself completely into its shell, which is hinged on the bottom for a tight seal. This is probably a male, since that sex tends to be more colorful. Most at home in marshes, bogs and small, secluded ponds, the spotted turtle is less often seen than the more obvious painted turtles and sliders.**

Massive – and threatened – the tortoises of the Galápagos Islands are descended from rather small species on the South American mainland. With no large grazers to compete for food, the tortoises evolved into giants as did unrelated tortoises on other islands scattered across the Pacific and Indian oceans.

And she waited. She was an ambush hunter, and understood patience on an instinctual level. Hours passed; dawn came, and behind it, a hot August day. Shaded by the tall trees, the rattler had no need to seek shelter from the sun, so she maintained her vigil, unmoving. Dusk came with the shrill, staccato cries of the katydids, which she did not hear, having no ears. But now, an hour before her second dawn, she feels through her jawbones the tickling vibration of a mouse scuttling along the log toward her.

Looking like a pancake with legs, a northern smooth softshelled turtle pokes its tubular nose above the surface for a breath. The softshell eats large quantities of insects and crayfish. Pausing at the entrance to a tunnel that may extend 30 feet underground, a gopher tortoise would seem to be safe from the hazards of the world above. Unfortunately, this Gulf States resident has declined significantly in the face of human development, and is endangered over much of its range. A female leatherback turtle climbs a beach in Malaysia to breed. The largest of the world's turtles, the leatherback can reach weights of nearly a ton, but egg collection has seriously hurt its population worldwide.

An American crocodile displays its impressive dentition; it is restricted to salt water and brackish water in extreme south Florida and the Keys, where it is an endangered species. *Below:* A Nile crocodile, a confirmed man-eater—in many parts of Africa it is more greatly feared than the lion. *Opposite:* The Siamese crocodile of Southeast Asia and the Malay Peninsula.

Opposite: Yacare caimans line a river in the Brazilian Pantanal, a vast wetlands system in South America's largest country. *Above:* The gavial (or gharial) has a needle-thin snout studded with teeth, a special adaptation for eating fish. Like most crocodilians, the gavial, found in India and neighboring countries, is endangered. *Below:* An American alligator in the tannin-stained waters of a southern swamp. Once endangered, it has responded so well to protection that legal hunting seasons are necessary to control their numbers.

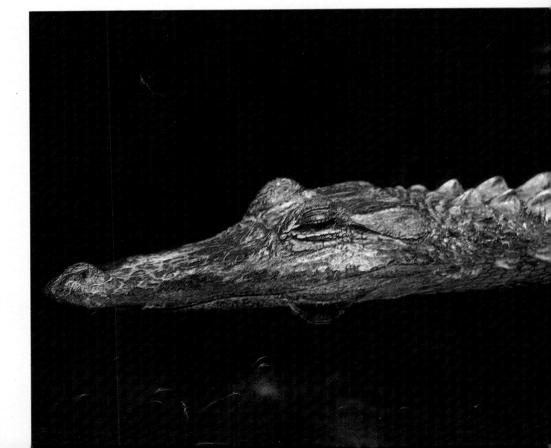

It is dim despite the moon, but the snake has no need of eyes. Her tongue flips in, out, in, out snaring information from the air and transferring it to a sensory organ in the roof of her mouth. And as the mouse nears, she can feel its body heat, through a pit between each nostril and eye. A moment later the mouse is abreast of her, and she strikes.

A Tokay, or Asian barking, gecko opens its mouth in a threat, although this small lizard is scarcely a danger. A quick swipe with its tongue keeps a Tokay's golden eyes clean of grit; special muscles open and close the zig-zagging pupil.

This page: The frilled lizard of Australia pulls an elaborate bluff to scare away predators. When gaping jaws don't work, the lizard can extend a ruff of skin around its neck, making it appear much bigger than it really is. *Overleaf:* Frozen in the light from a high-speed flash, an African chameleon lunges toward its prey, even as its long, sticky tongue lashes out to snag the butterfly. The movement is over in a split second, almost too fast for the eye to follow.

Preceding page & this page: The changing colors of a chameleon are in response to environmental conditions rather than a conscious attempt to mimic the background. Here, a broken fern frond on a chameleon's back blocks the sun, and leaves a silhouette underneath.

Looking like a monster-movie extra, a tri-horned chameleon clambers over a flower, its bulbous eyes swiveling independently as it hunts for insects. *Below:* An adult Jackson's chameleon unwittingly carries a hitchhiker — a juvenile of the same species.

The motion is over in a flash — mouth open, hinged fangs swinging forward and locking into place, the impact driving the needles into the mouse's flanks, and a muscular contraction around twin venom glands. Then the rattler pulls back, all in the blink of an eye, and waits again.

The mouse dies quickly, its body overcome by the massive dose of poison. Following its tongue and pits once again, the snake eases forward to where the dead rodent is, and begins to swallow. Unable to chew, it simply engulfs its prey whole, headfirst, unhinging its lower jaws from its skull so the elastic skin of its mouth and throat can stretch around the mouse. Ten minutes later the mouse is an anonymous lump in the rattlesnake's midsection, and the snake will not have to feed again for a week or so.

A harmless member of the iguanid group, the double-crested basilisk of Central America is named for the mythical basilisk, whose very gaze was said to kill.

Reptiles and amphibians have an ancient lineage, but they are by no means primitive. A rattlesnake has been finely honed by natural selection for a life of hunting warmblooded prey through the night; so, too, has evolution molded the bullfrog for the marsh, the crocodile for the tropical delta, the sea turtle for the open ocean and the lizard for the barren desert. They represent a handful of themes but thousands of variations, each exquisitely right for a particular place and lifestyle.

The amphibians are the older of the two, an evolutionary step beyond fish. They first appeared some 350 million years ago, with two major changes to fish anatomy – what had been pectoral and ventral fins were modified into stumpy legs, and air chambers in the body, once used for equilibrium while swimming, became the original version of lungs. Thus equipped, they took the land by storm. . .or at least at a sedate waddle.

This page: Commonly sold in pet stores as "chameleons," the green anole is not related to the true Old World chameleon. The green anole blends nicely with the vegetation of its Southeastern home. Colors can change from green to brown and blotchy intergrades of the two, determined not by the scenery, but by the temperature and the anole's condition. Sleeping anoles, for instance, are usually bright green. Shedding skin peels off in gray sheets, which the anole will probably eat. The frequency of shedding depends on how fast it grows.

Two collared lizards—the male is the more colorful of the pair. Like most lizards they are solitary except in the mating season. Known in some areas of the U.S. as "mountain boomers," even though they are silent, collared lizards run erect on their hind feet, using their long tails for balance just as bipedal dinosaurs did. *Below:* Elongated toes help the New World cone-headed lizard to scramble through the tropical treetops.

Today amphibians come in several varieties: the salamanders, which most closely resemble the ancestral amphibians; frogs and toads, with their adaptations for hopping rather than walking; and the little-known caecilians, legless, often blind burrowers that resemble nothing so much as earthworms.

When the first amphibians crawled ashore, they found a world ripe for the picking, overflowing with insects for food but with no vertebrates beyond themselves. As with any group of animals confronting a new environment, they diverged to fill most of the available niches; some early salamanders reached lengths of 13 feet. But successful as they were, the amphibians had one major drawback—their dependence on water.

The common iguana—a common lizard in Central and South America—is edible. Some entrepreneurs now raise them commercially. A female common iguana stands among her clutch of eggs, which can expect scant attention from her.

A Galápagos iguana shows hints of its green iguana ancestors, but has been changed by natural selection to fit the harsh environment of the islands. *Below:* A lava lizard, its spiky scales reflective of the hard life on a desert island, is native to Hood Island in the Galápagos chain.

An amphibian's skin isn't watertight. If the atmosphere is dry and the animal is away from water, or if it is caught in bright sun, it will dehydrate rapidly, condemned to death by moisture loss. For this reason, amphibians prefer wet places like marshes, swamps, the damp forest floor, the undersides of flat rocks – any place where they can absorb vital water through their skin. A few, like the spadefoot toads of the Southwest and the water-holding frog of Australia, have partially overcome this hurdle by spending most of their lives underground, buried in moist sand, coming up only at night, or after a rain.

Water is also essential for amphibian reproduction. All amphibians lay eggs covered in a gelatinous coating –"frog jelly" to any child who's picked up a mass of slimy frog eggs. But such protection is scanty, especially against desiccation, and as a result almost all amphibian eggs are

Top to bottom: On Hood Island, a marine iguana suns itself after diving in the frigid water for seaweed. The dorsal spikes on the neck and back of this green iguana help deter predators, although its agility is probably of greater value. Marine iguanas warm themselves on Punta Espinosa in the Galápagos. Descended from the same species as the land iguana, the marine iguana has developed the ability to dive to extreme depths for long periods of time. *Overleaf:* The Galápagos marine iguana has special glands in its nasal cavities to expel the excess salt from its blood – salt that would otherwise quickly kill it.

laid in water. Development is generally swift, particularly among those species that breed in temporary pools, like rain puddles in the desert and pools of spring snowmelt in the East. The gilled larvae hatch after a matter of weeks, days or even hours, and generally do not look like their parents.

Frogs and toads begin, of course, as tadpoles. When an American toad emerges from its egg, the tadpole is barely recognizable as such – a tiny, flattened black blob with a tail and external gills, but no eyes and only a tubular mouth. That quickly changes, and within days the tadpole has eyes, a round head and distinct tail. Its mouth and digestive system are geared for a vegetarian diet of algae and aquatic plants, and it eats

Top to bottom: **A Clark's spiny lizard is ready in an instant to vanish among the rocks of its Arizona desert home. Horny serrations on the toes of the fringed-toed lizard of the American Southwest help it to walk on loose sand. Among the mountain dragon lizards of Thailand, another tree-dwelling species, only the male has a well-developed crest and throat fan, used for bluffing rivals.** *Opposite:* **The five-lined skink is found from New England to Florida and west to the Great Plains. This is an adult male, told by the reddish color of the head; juveniles of both sexes have electric-blue tails.**

A western skink displays the smooth, almost slippery scales and blunt head of this wide-ranging family. *Below:* This Australian blue-tongued skink seems scarcely equipped for movement; its tongue is deep blue, for unknown reasons.

constantly, growing at a rate determined by the water temperature; for this reason, polliwogs raised in a warm home, then returned to the marsh, will be quite a bit bigger than their stay-at-home siblings.

How long the frog or toad remains a tadpole depends on the species; spadefoot toads metamorphose in a few weeks, other toads, a few months. Bullfrogs have the longest larval period of any North American frog, up to three years in northern regions. The hind legs, sprouting from what are known as "limb buds," appear first, and the tail begins to shorten as it is reabsorbed into the tadpole's body. Later, front legs appear, growing out of what had been the tadpole's gill openings. Even more dramatic changes are occurring inside the creature's body. The gut is shortened, permitting a diet of meat instead of plants; the small, circular mouth stretches

Top to bottom: **The emerald lizard, a southern European species with a mosaic of colorful scales. The Italian wall lizard, a common species from Spain to the Black Sea, long puzzled scientists with its wide variety of color phases, especially among isolated island populations. This small black tegu will grow into an efficient hunter of wild birds, small mammals, and domestic poultry—earning the name "chicken wolf" in South America.**

and widens, growing a long tongue. The gills are replaced by lungs, which grow from air pouches. In many ways, the metamorphosis of a tadpole mirrors the evolutionary development from fish to amphibian.

Salamanders also produce larvae, although they are not commonly known as tadpoles. Like the frog larvae, the young salamanders have gills, in their case large, feathery organs alongside the head. The salamander larvae are predatory from the start, and are born with legs, so their metamorphosis is not as dramatic. A few, in fact, have

Black tongue probing for the scent of food – a clutch of bird eggs, perhaps, or a nest of mice – the Gila monster is one of only two poisonous lizards in the world, the Gila monster is really an inoffensive creature, now sadly reduced in numbers due to overcollecting. *Below:* **At home on land or in the water, the Nile monitor feeds on fish, frogs and shellfish, but is especially fond of crocodile eggs, dug up from their nests on sandy riverbanks.**

dispensed with life on land altogether. The mudpuppies and waterdogs are permanent larvae, never losing their gills.

A few groups of amphibians lay their eggs out of the water, including some North American salamanders, which lay them under rotting logs, and several unique frogs and toads. The midwife toad of Europe actually carries its string of eggs wrapped around its hind legs, hobbling from pool to pool, while some tropical species create a froth of bubbles in the treetops in which to lay.

But even then, the amphibians are making the best of a bad reproductive situation. The approach taken by the reptiles is far more efficient. Reptiles have sealed themselves – and their eggs – in a watertight case. A reptile's skin is thick and dry, resistant to drought. Just as important, its eggs are encased in a

Majestic in its bulk, a Komodo dragon may reach lengths of 12 feet, feeding on carrion, goats, pigs and deer. It is the largest lizard in the world, and although its reputation for ferocity is overstated, it is nonetheless an impressive animal. *Right:* Throat puffed in anger, a Merten's water monitor bluffs a challenge. Those in Australia today are mere reflections of giant goannas that lived on the island continent until the last ice age, when they reach lengths of 21 feet and weights of 1,300 pounds.

Draped in characteristic loops over branch, this young emerald tree boa will undergo a remarkable color transformation as it grows, replacing the orange with a vivid emerald-green that matches the South American rain forest canopy where it lives.

leathery shell, and do not have to be laid in a moist place. No wonder the reptiles quickly supplanted amphibians as the dominant form of vertebrate life.

How to tell a reptile from an amphibian at glance? Reptiles have scales or plates, and the toes (if present) have claws. Amphibians have no scales (the skin is usually moist, but not always) and no claws.

It has become a cliché to say that reptiles "ruled the Earth," but they did, for far longer than mankind's brief existence. The age of dinosaurs, considered the pinnacle of reptilian evolution, lasted for nearly 100 million years. Then, at the end of the Cretaceous Period some 65 million years ago, the dinosaurs became extinct in one of the periodic "great dyings," the mass extinctions that mark the planet's history. Whether as a result of gradual climatic change or Earth's collision

Top to bottom: **An adult emerald tree boa prepares to strike. A treetop hunter, this boa feeds primarily on birds; it kills its prey, not by crushing it but by squeezing in each time its prey exhales, until the animal can no longer breathe. Small for a boa, the rough-scaled sand boa is a burrower in the deserts of India and nearby regions. Adapted to its harsh environment, this species is more tolerant of high temperatures than most snakes.**

with an asteroid, the results were unequivocal – the dinosaurs were gone. (Or at least, the dinosaurs as we usually think of them were gone. One compelling theory holds that birds are their direct descendants, and some paleontologists have even gone so far as to suggest lumping birds and dinosaurs in the same taxonomic class, Dinosauria.)

Maroon and white highlights mark this juvenile green tree python, another arboreal constrictor from the tropics. *Below:* A subspecies of the Indian python, the Burmese python is strikingly patterned, making juveniles prized by snake collectors. *Opposite:* An adult green tree python waits for a meal in New Guinea.

A few major reptile groups survived the extinctions, however – the crocodilians, turtles, lizards and snakes, and a single species in a fifth group, the lizard-like tuatara of New Zealand. Turtles in particular are often referred to as "living fossils," as though they somehow muddled through to this point by accident, having outlived their day. Nothing could be further from the truth; every plant and animal species alive today survives because it is perfectly suited to its environment and capable of changing when the environment changes.

The scarlet kingsnake of the American Southeast mimics the poisonous coral snake's red, yellow and black colors, but not its pattern; in the coral snake, the red and yellow bands touch. The speckled kingsnake is a common constrictor of the Mississippi Valley and eastern Great Plains, where it hunts birds, small mammals, reptiles and amphibians. *Opposite:* Three longitudinal lines, one light and two dark, make this eastern garter snake easy to identify.

Preceding pages: The corn snake (also known as the red rat snake) is one of the prettiest reptiles in the U.S., with its rich orange markings and an iridescent sheen that makes the skin look oily. *Opposite:* Looking like a vine or branch, the climbing rat snake of Thailand is colored perfectly for its life among the trees. *This page:* When is a black snake not black? When it is a baby, like these hatchling black rat snakes emerging from their eggs. The grayish pattern will darken as the snakes mature, but even a 5-foot adult will show vestiges of its infant markings. The rare Everglades rat snake is a member of a highly variable species, differing greatly in color depending on where it is found. This orangish race occurs only in extreme southern Florida.

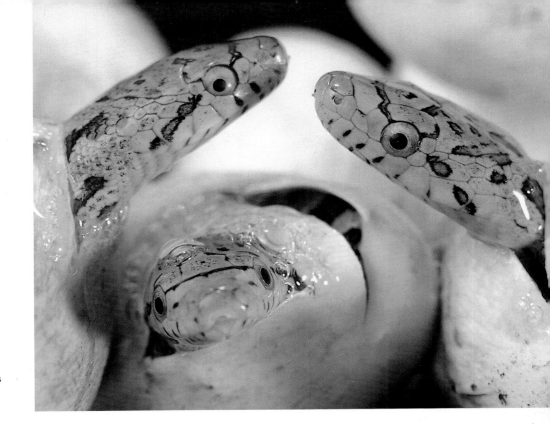

A smooth green snake flicks out its tongue—and in the process, learns a great deal about the world around it. The tongue picks up odor particles from the air and transfers them to a specialized sensing organ in the roof of the mouth, giving the snake information about nearby food, water and danger. *Below:* On the high plains of Texas, a female bullsnake lays another egg in her still-unfinished clutch. Encased in a leathery shell, a reptile egg can survive on land, giving reptiles far more flexibility in their habitat. *Opposite:* The largest poisonous snake in the world, the king cobra of Asia sometimes exceeds 12 feet in length, but is shy and rarely a threat to humans. Its lethal venom is normally reserved for its prey, lizards and smaller snakes.

Common in the grain fields of India, where it feeds on rodents, Russell's viper is one of the leading culprits in snakebite deaths in that country.

Turtles, protected by their thick shells, hit on a body plan that works, and had no need to do anything more than tinker with the details.

If reptiles have a survival drawback, it is their metabolism. Like amphibians, reptiles are ectothermic, "cold-blooded" – unable to sustain a body temperature much different from that of their surroundings. On a cold day, a reptile is sluggish, unable to move quickly or digest food, and a hard freeze may kill it, which is why reptiles have not colonized the coldest parts of the world. Likewise, direct, broiling sun can be fatal just as quickly. So reptiles adjust their body temperature by changing their location, moving from shade to sun and back again to keep an optimum level. In winter they must hibernate below the frost line.

Top to bottom: **Pinker, with narrower bands than its northern cousin, the southern copperhead is found from Virginia south to Florida in woodlands and swamps. Newborn northern copperheads curl next to their mother's body moments after birth. Like the garter snakes, rattlesnakes and several other species, copperheads retain the eggs inside the female's body until they are ready to hatch. The awe-inspiring, venomous Gaboon viper of tropical Africa has been known to eat monkeys and small antelope. Squat and heavy, it has the longest fangs of any snake.**

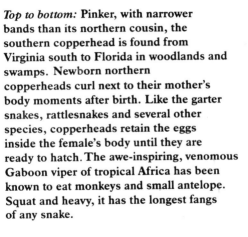

Flashing a warning with its open, white mouth, a cottonmouth stands its ground, ready to bite if pushed too far. A common pit viper of southern swamps, marshes and wet fields, it feeds primarily on small reptiles and amphibians. A resting cottonmouth shows the pit, between the eye and nostril, that gives the pit viper group its name. A heat-sensing organ, the pit helps the snake find and track its prey in the dark.

(Again, new research suggests that we must alter our image of dinosaurs, which may have developed endothermy – "warm-bloodedness"– millions of years ago, and passed it on to mammals and birds.) And for this same metabolic reason, reptiles are most common and diverse in hot climates – the tropics and deserts.

The crocodilians – crocodiles, alligators, caimans and their relatives – are the largest surviving reptiles; saltwater crocodiles have been known to reach 20 feet and one is recorded at nearly 28 feet. Most are far smaller, however. The American alligator, habitué of swamps and sloughs, is big at 12 feet, and rare at 16, while the critically endangered American crocodile, restricted to salt and brackish water, generally runs the same size. In general, crocs have longer, thinner snouts than alligators and caimans, and the longest, thinnest of all belongs to the gharial, or gavial, of India, with its needle-like face.

Leaving its trademark tracks, a sidewinder moves across loose sand by throwing a loop of its body forward, then bracing itself for another throw. While this Southwestern rattlesnake is best known for this motion, most snakes will "sidewind" on a surface with poor traction. Reaching lengths of about 25 inches, the sidewinder is also known as the horned rattlesnake, because of the scales that project above the eyes.

Opposite: One of the midgets of the pit viper clan, the dusky pygmy rattlesnake of the Southeast has a rattle that sounds like the buzz of an insect. Rarely longer than a foot and a half, the dusky pygmy preys on frogs, lizards and mice. *Above:* Contrary to popular belief, rattlesnakes—like this prairie rattler in Texas—do not always rattle before striking. It seems likely that the rattle arose during the Pleistocene, as a way of warning off herds of grazing animals that would otherwise trample the snake. *Right:* The largest venomous snake in North America, the eastern diamond-back rattlesnake may reach lengths of 8 feet. Because of its size—and thus the amount of venom it can inject with a bite—and its adaptability to populated areas, it's ranked as one of the most dangerous snakes in the U.S.

Of all the reptiles except sea turtles, crocodilians have suffered the most at the hands of man. Worldwide, millions have been killed for leather, meat or eggs, and 20 species or subspecies are listed as threatened or endangered. The American alligator has responded so well to protection that legal hunting seasons are again allowed, and other species are following suit, now that controls on the killing have been put in place.

Turtles are the most unusual of all reptiles, "carrying their home on their backs," as the old saying goes. The shell has two parts, the carapace (or upper shell) and plastron. Covered with large scales called laminae, the shells are made of fused bones, and are correspondingly hard. Turtles completely lack teeth, having instead a horny beak.

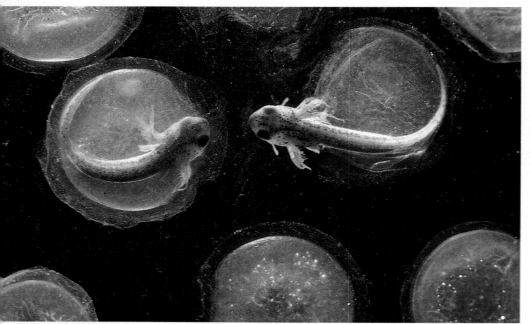

Top to bottom: **The spotted salamander, a burrowing species common from southern California to the Gulf, is one of the earliest breeders each spring, emerging from muddy pond bottoms sometimes before the ice has even melted from the surface. Inside the globular egg mass, the larvae develop quickly, emerging with gills.**

Flip a rock or rotting log along a streambank, and you're liable to find a long-tailed salamander. Quick and surprisingly agile, the salamander will bolt for cover almost immediately, diving into the water if possible. *Below:* A mole salamander like the spotted, beautifully marked marbled salamander breeds in small vernal ponds of snowmelt and rainwater, putting it at risk from rising levels of acid rain.

Generally speaking, a turtle that lives on land is called a tortoise, and if in the water, a turtle, but the rule is often broken, as with the terrestrial box turtles, probably the most familiar turtles in North America. Box turtles are among the few that can almost completely retreat inside their shells, thanks to a hinge across the front third of the plastron. Confronted with danger, the box turtle pulls in its head and legs and clamps the plastron shut. A persistent predator may be able to get a few nips at the turtle's hind legs (which don't fit inside totally), but usually it will give up in disgust.

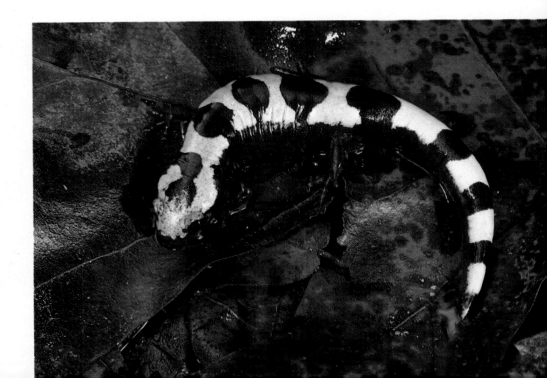

Of the world's reptiles, more than half – about 3,000 species – are lizards. They range from the diminutive to the dinosaur-like, the latter being the Komodo "dragon" of Indonesia, a whopping 12 feet long and decidedly carnivorous in its diet. As a group, lizards are the most active of the reptiles, as anyone who has tried to catch a racerunner, anole or fence lizard has quickly discovered. Some, like the collard lizard of the United States, can run on their hind legs like miniature dinosaurs, while others, such as the glass lizard of the Southeast, have lost their legs entirely.

One of several distinctly marked salamanders found in the mountains that divide the Carolinas, Georgia and Tennessee, the red-legged salamander is now considered a subspecies of the red-cheeked salamander. *Below:* The northern dusky salamander of the East can lay its clutch of white eggs on land, hidden beneath rocks and logs where the embryos will not dry out.

This 6-inch-long northern red salamander will fade to a dull purple as it ages. It haunts woodland springs and mountain streams from the Appalachians to New England.
Below: One of the large group of North American species called plethodons, or lungless salamanders, the slimy salamander absorbs oxygen through its damp skin. Its name comes from a sticky skin secretion that repels predators.

A lizard without legs is not a snake; legless lizards have eyelids and external ears, which snakes lack, as well as a number of internal differences not obvious at first glance. But snakes did apparently evolve from lizards, about 100 million years ago. The lack of legs might seem a step backwards (pun intended), but it is not the drawback it appears. Snakes can move in several ways: a caterpillarish crawl using the large belly scales, the common undulating slither, and "sidewinding" on loose surfaces like sand, in which a loop of the body is thrown sideways, anchored and used a brace to pull the rest of the snake up to it.

The brilliant underside of the Oriental fire-bellied toad of eastern China serves notice to birds and other predators — this amphibian's skin secretions are toxic. By advertising the fact, the toad avoids attacks that might injure it, even though the attacker would also be anticipated. *Left:* A pug-nosed eastern spadefoot toad sits on its distinguishing field mark — a horny, comma-shaped "spade" on each hind foot that lets it dig itself straight down into loose soil. *Opposite:* The "long-nosed" form of the Malayan horned frog has flaps of skin over the nose and each eye, flaps that are highly sensitive to touch.

The heavyweight among North American frogs, the bullfrog is the common "jug-o-rum" of summer ponds and marshes. Slow-growing bullfrogs take up to three years to change from tadpole to adult; once transformed, they continue to grow as long as they live, which can be 16 years.

Snakes have fascinated people for millennia and have figured in history, religion and myth – the serpent in the Garden of Eden, the asp that Cleopatra used to commit suicide, for example. Even if the mixture of attraction and repellency never go away, at least many of the old falsehoods about snakes have. Snakes are not slimy, but dry as leather; they do not bite without provocation; they cannot sting with their tongue or tail; they do not hypnotize their prey. There are enough remarkable facts about snakes without the embellishments of fiction. The rattle of a rattlesnake, for example, is not intended to give gentlemanly warning, as once thought, but to keep the snake alive.

Top to bottom: **A green frog peeks from a concealing blanket of duckweed, viewing the world through its gilded eyes. The European edible frog is the first choice for a meal of frog legs. It is a member of the widespread genus *Rana,* to which the North American green frog, bullfrog and leopard frog belong. An American toad belts out his song of love to a nighttime marsh, his buzzy trill resonating in his inflated vocal sac.** *Overleaf:* **Two dart-poison frogs from Costa Rica. Many frogs and toads secrete bitter substances from their skin to thwart predators, but what oozes from a dart-poison frog can be deadly if ingested.**

Rattlers evolved during the Pleistocene, when North America was awash with huge herds of grazing animals. Many snakes buzz their tails when angry; the rattlers developed loose scales on the tail tip that magnified the sound, warning away bison, horses, and camels – and their dangerous hooves.

As science continues to probe beyond the misconceptions that surround reptiles and amphibians, it paints a picture of a remarkable set of animals, living in harmony with their environment, molded by it into endlessly amazing forms. Fortunately, more and more people are looking beyond the myths of the past and discovering for themselves this fascinating part of the natural world.

Dendrobates pumilio, one of the most common dart-poison frogs, is found from Nicaragua to Panama. Most are red with dark blue legs, but in the Panama region they may be green, yellow or other colors. *Below:* The flamboyant colors of these frogs serve as a warning to potential predators. The Choco Indians of Colombia use the deadly secretions to tip their darts with one of the deadliest toxins in nature.

This page: The harlequin frog of Central America; this is *Atelopus varius*, a species from Costa Rica. A blue dart-poison frog amid the greenery of Suriname.

Enlarged, adhesive toepads give this giant treefrog of the New World tropics excellent purchase. Swelled to bursting, a barking treefrog calls from a South Carolina swamp. This species has two distinct calls: the breeding call and the more common bark. *Opposite:* A red-eyed treefrog from Costa Rica has enlarged orbs for better night vision.

Index of Photography

TIB = The Image Bank